Magic,Myth & Monsters:
A Fantasy Coloring book

Issue #2
Created by Steven Fenczik

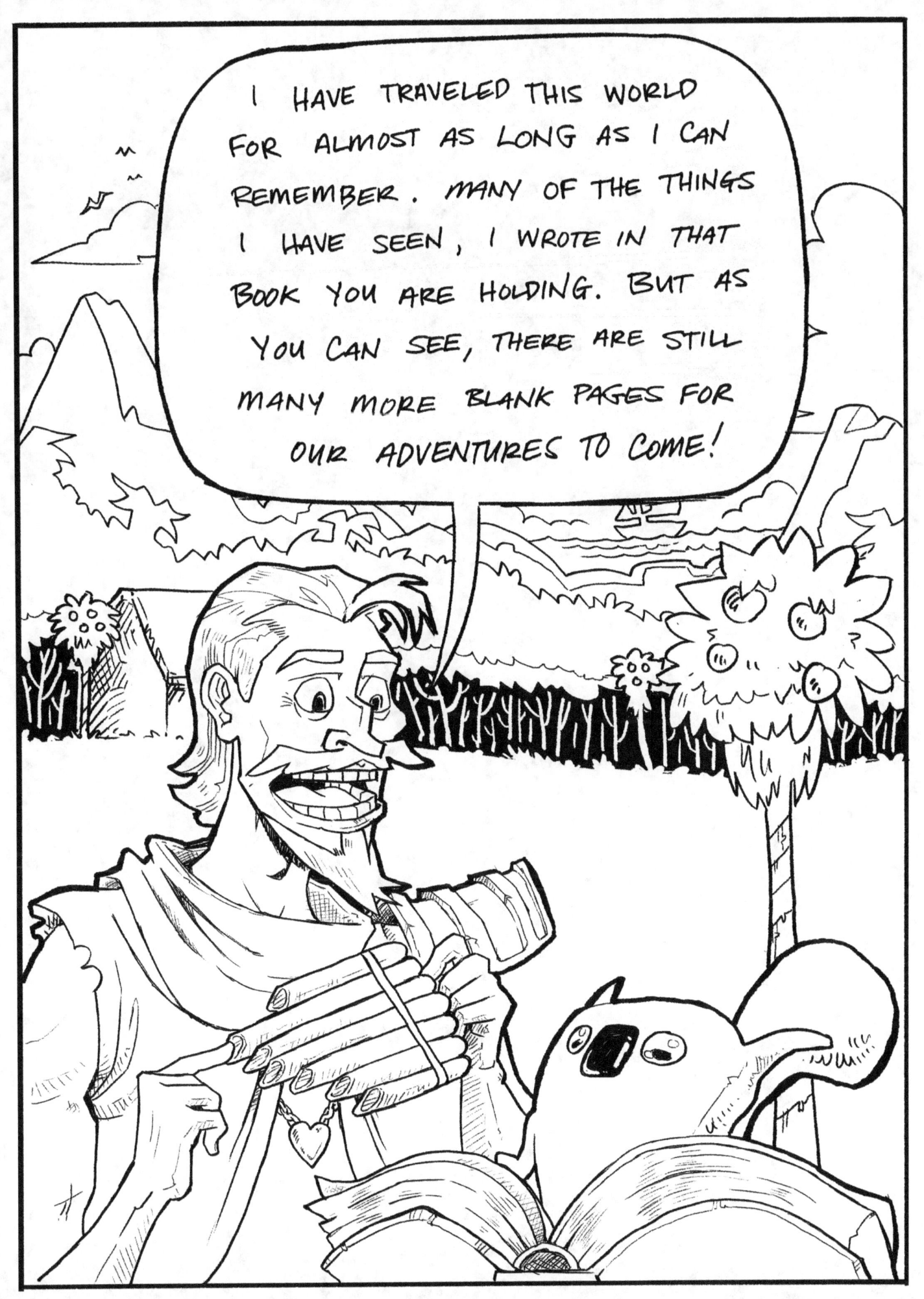

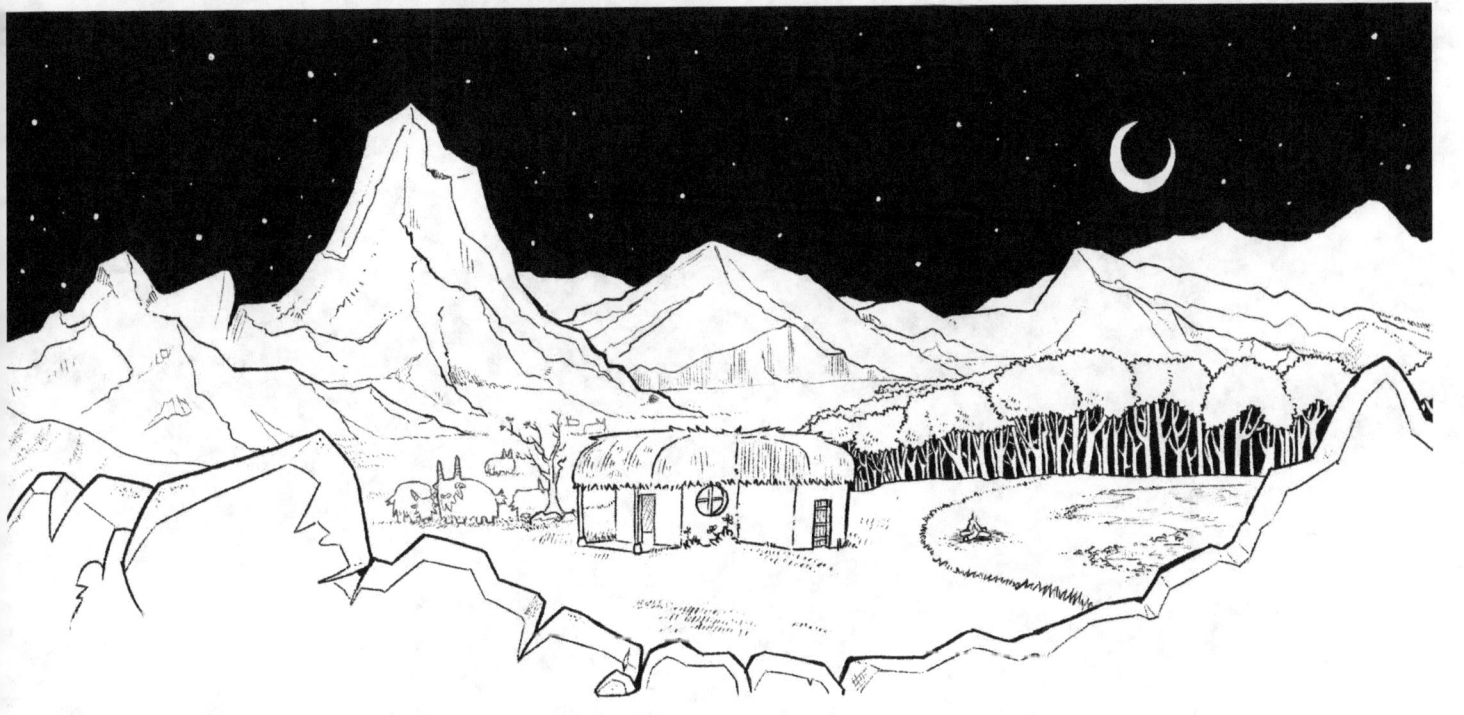

Prior to travelling the world, I was a shepherd.
I tended to a group of Moon Yaks deep in
the southern mountains. They say that
when the wind blows the music of
the local spirits bounces from peak to peak.

That was a long time ago...
Now my life is with you Ooby my boy. Travelling
the world, telling tales, and singing songs from
days of yore.

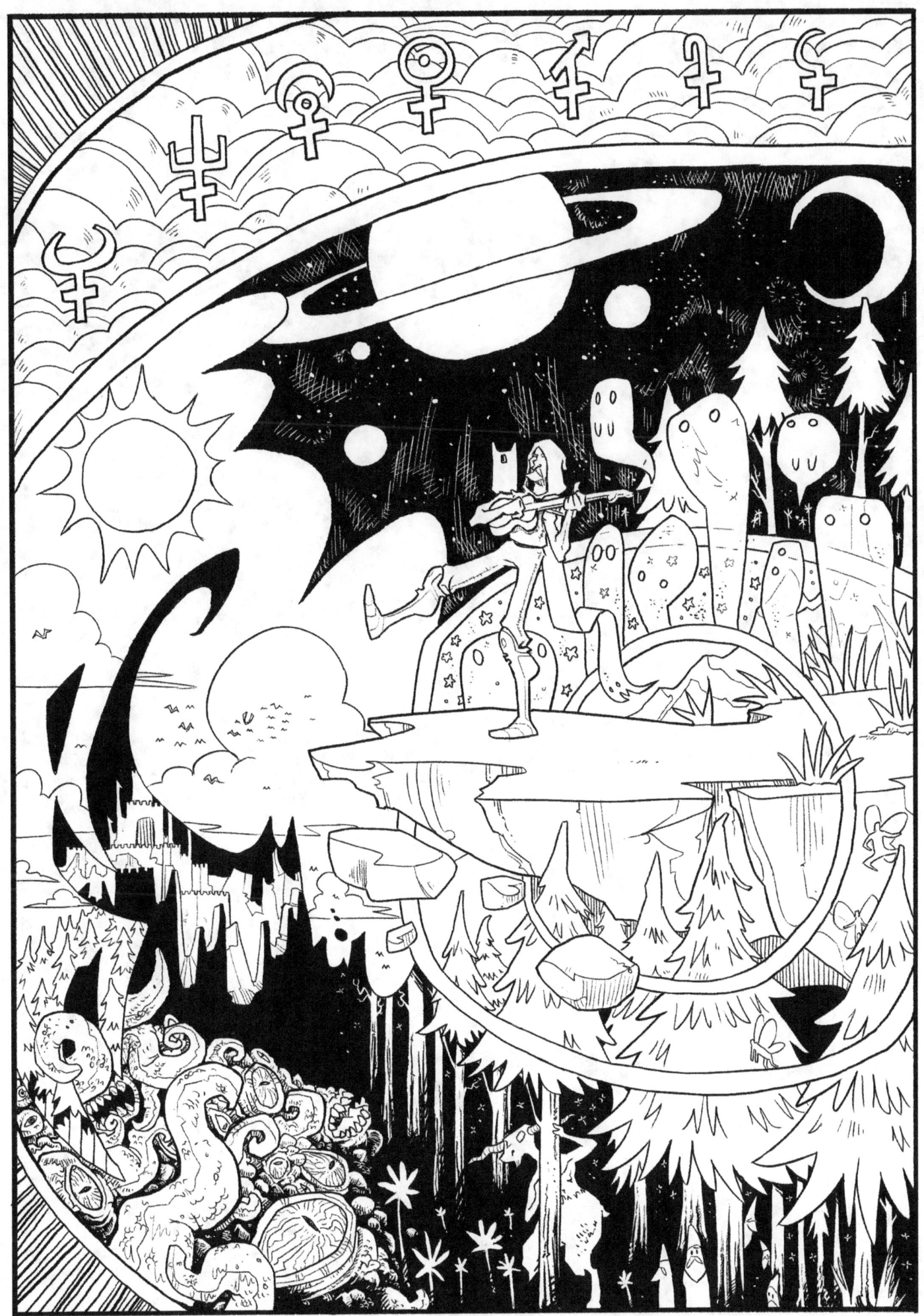

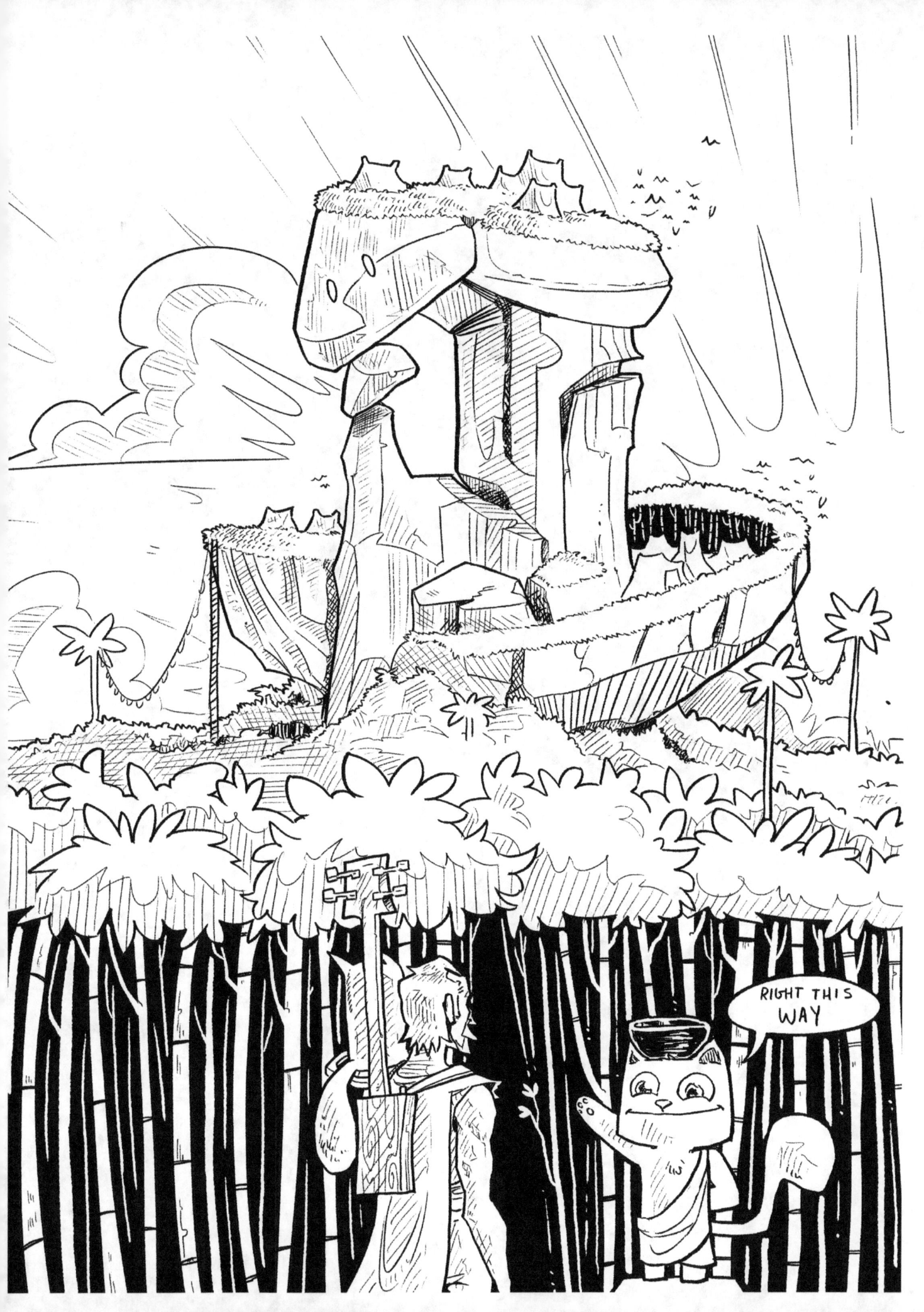

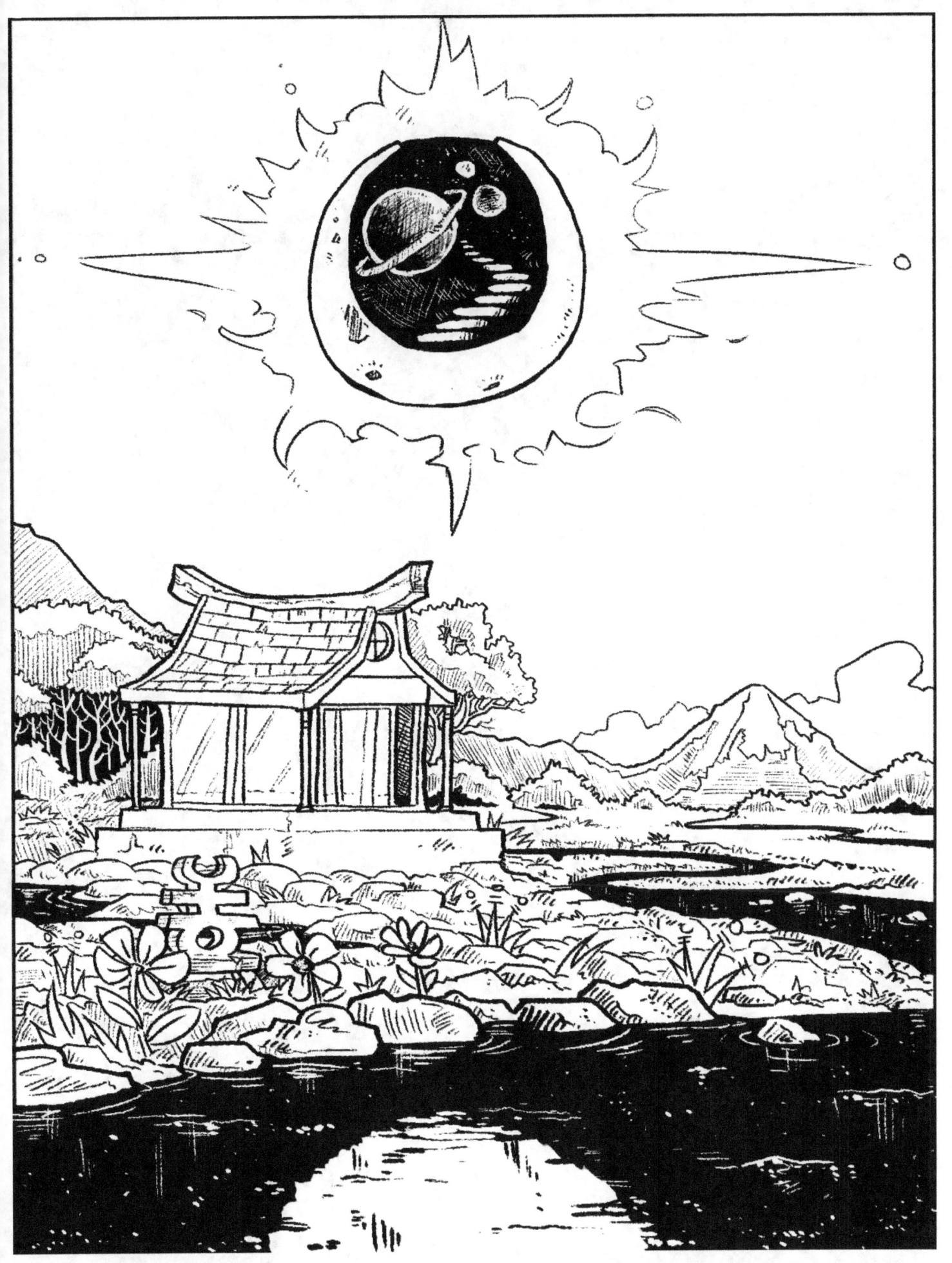

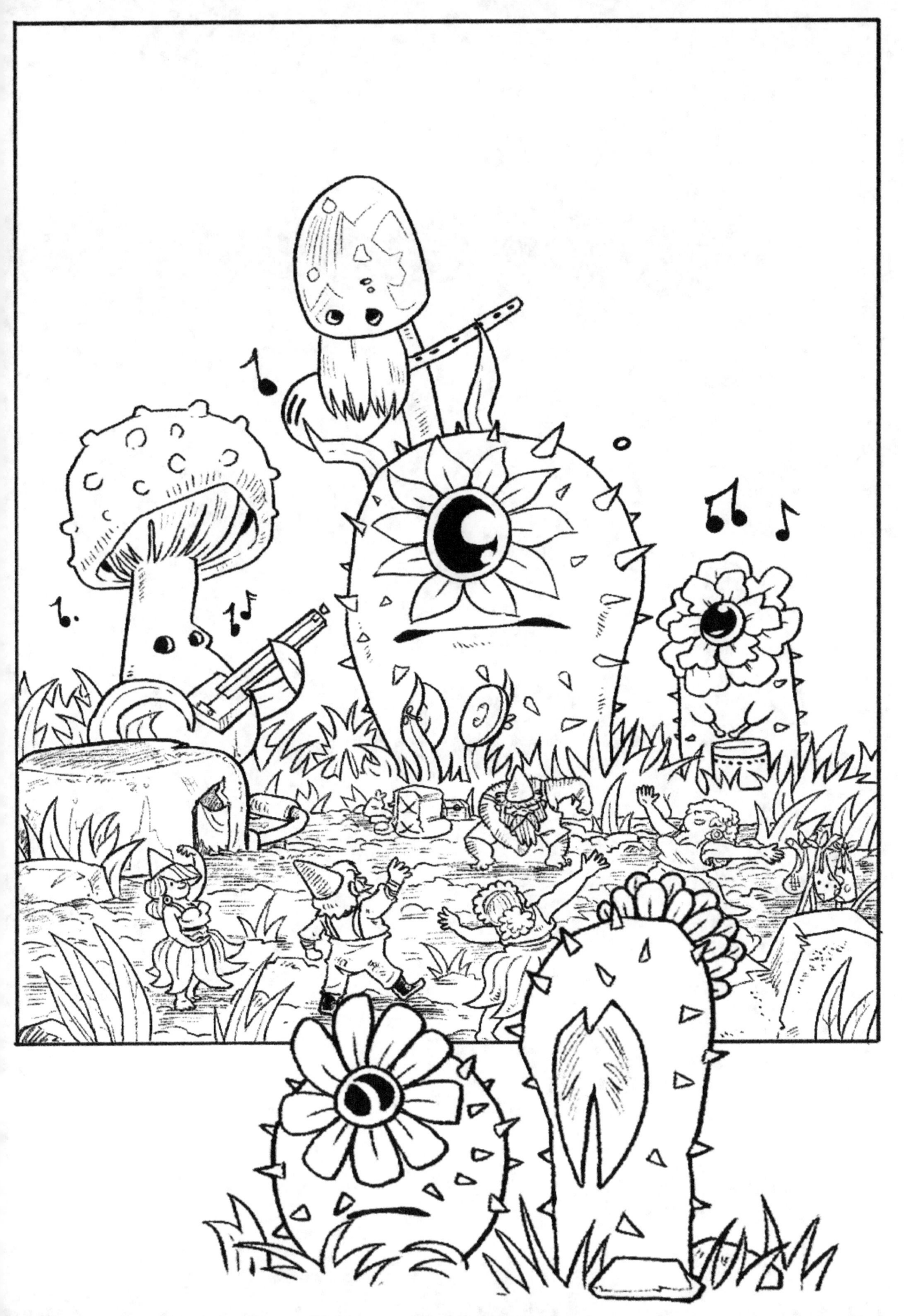

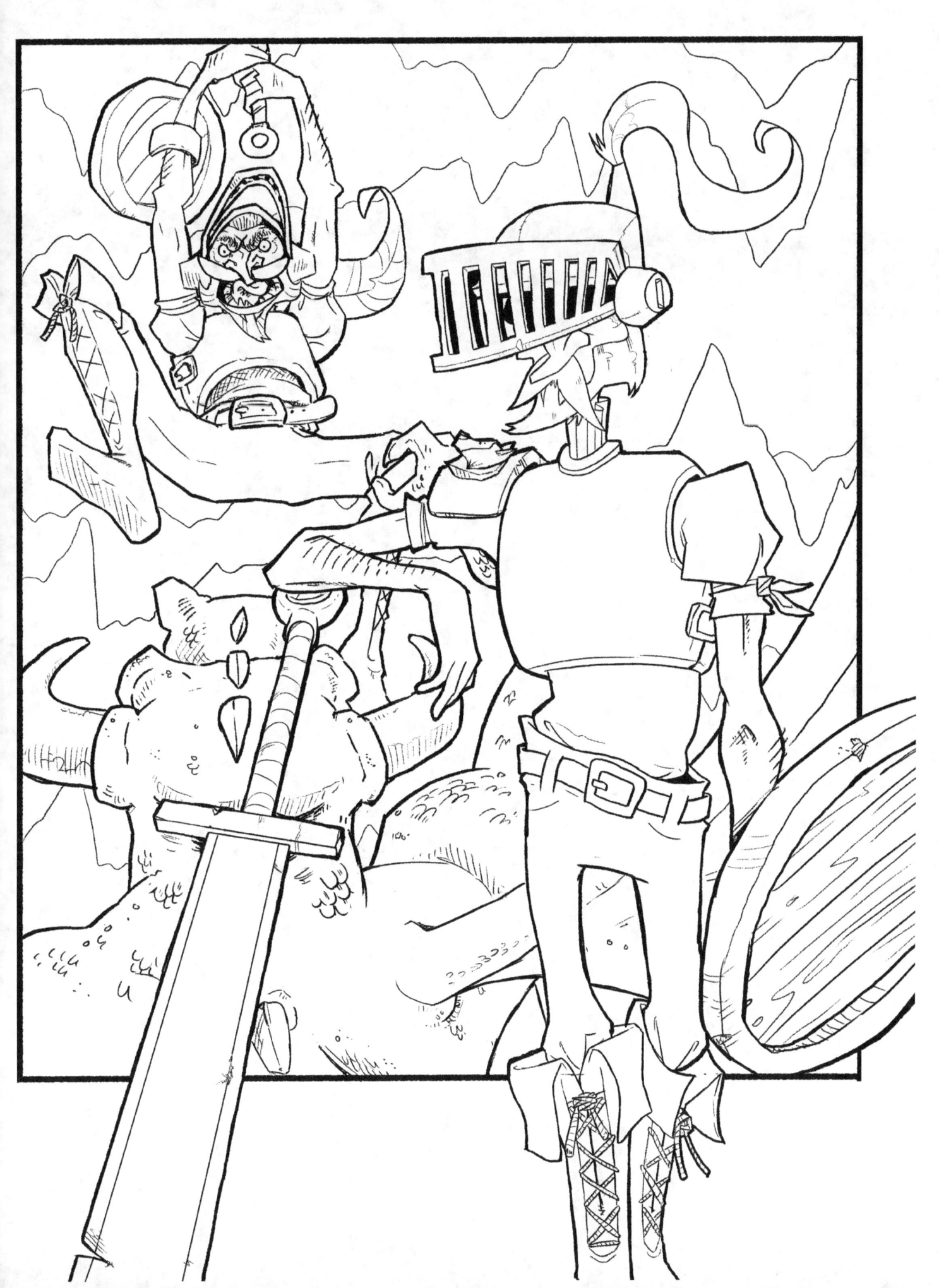

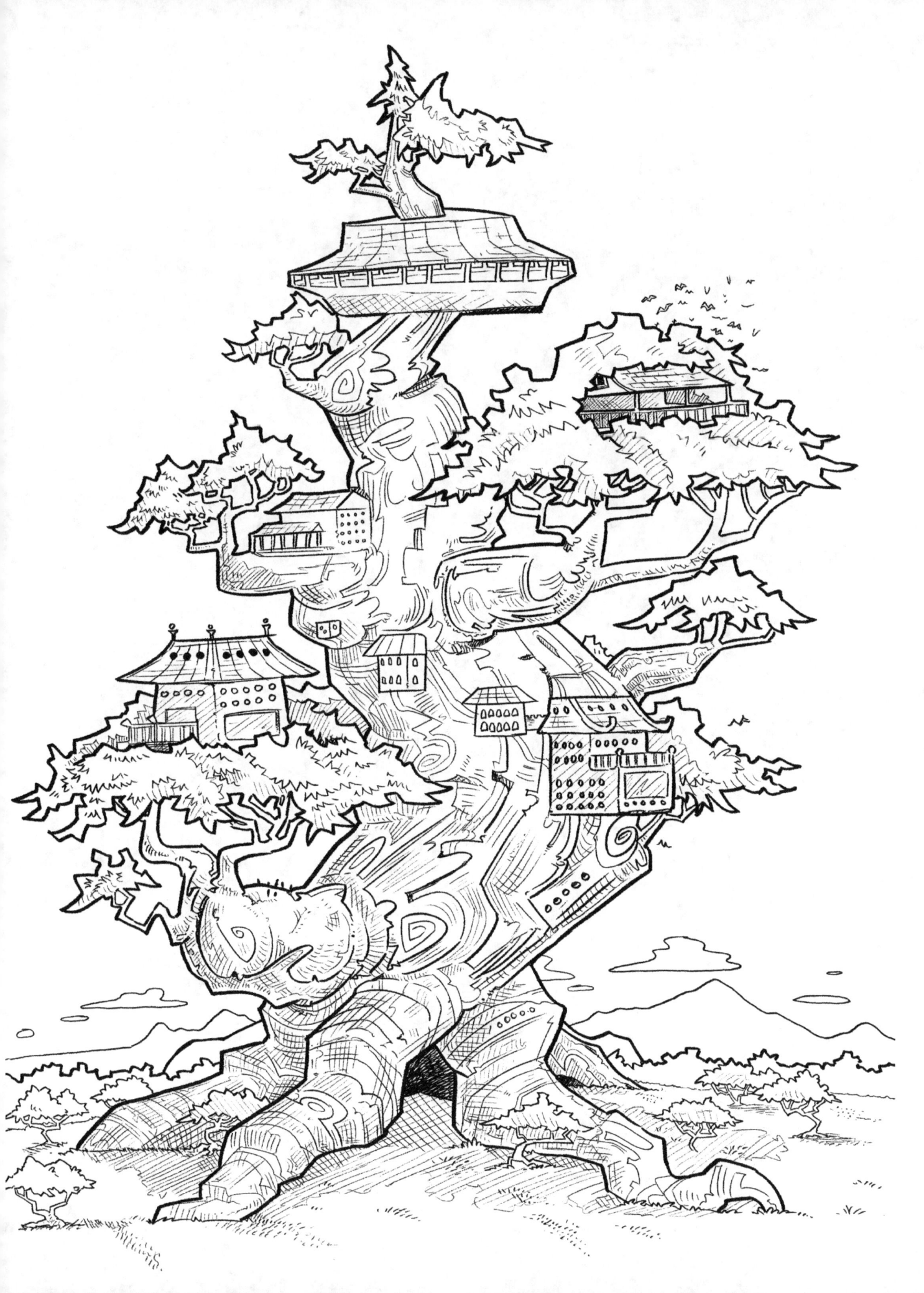

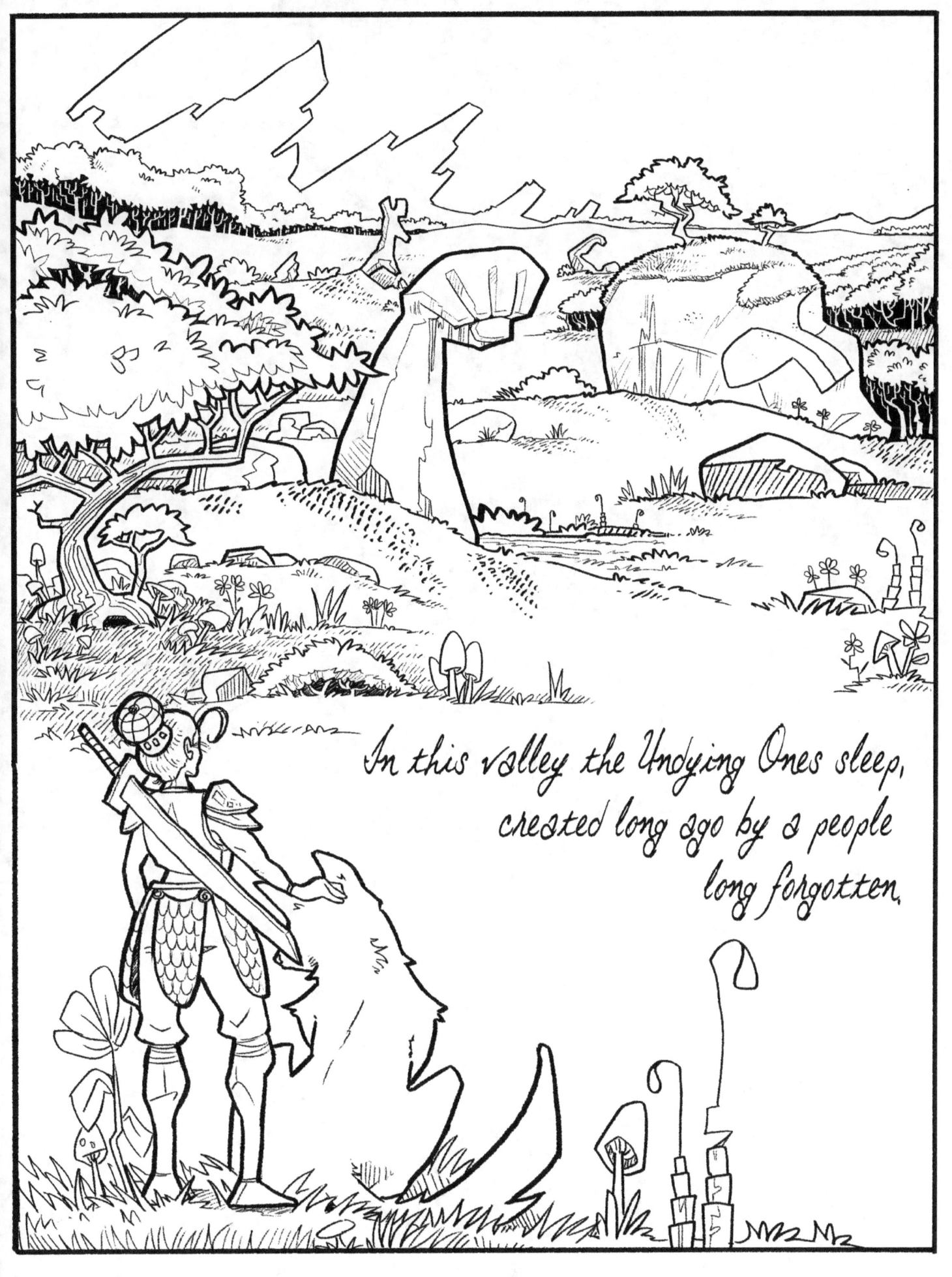

In this valley the Undying Ones sleep, created long ago by a people long forgotten.

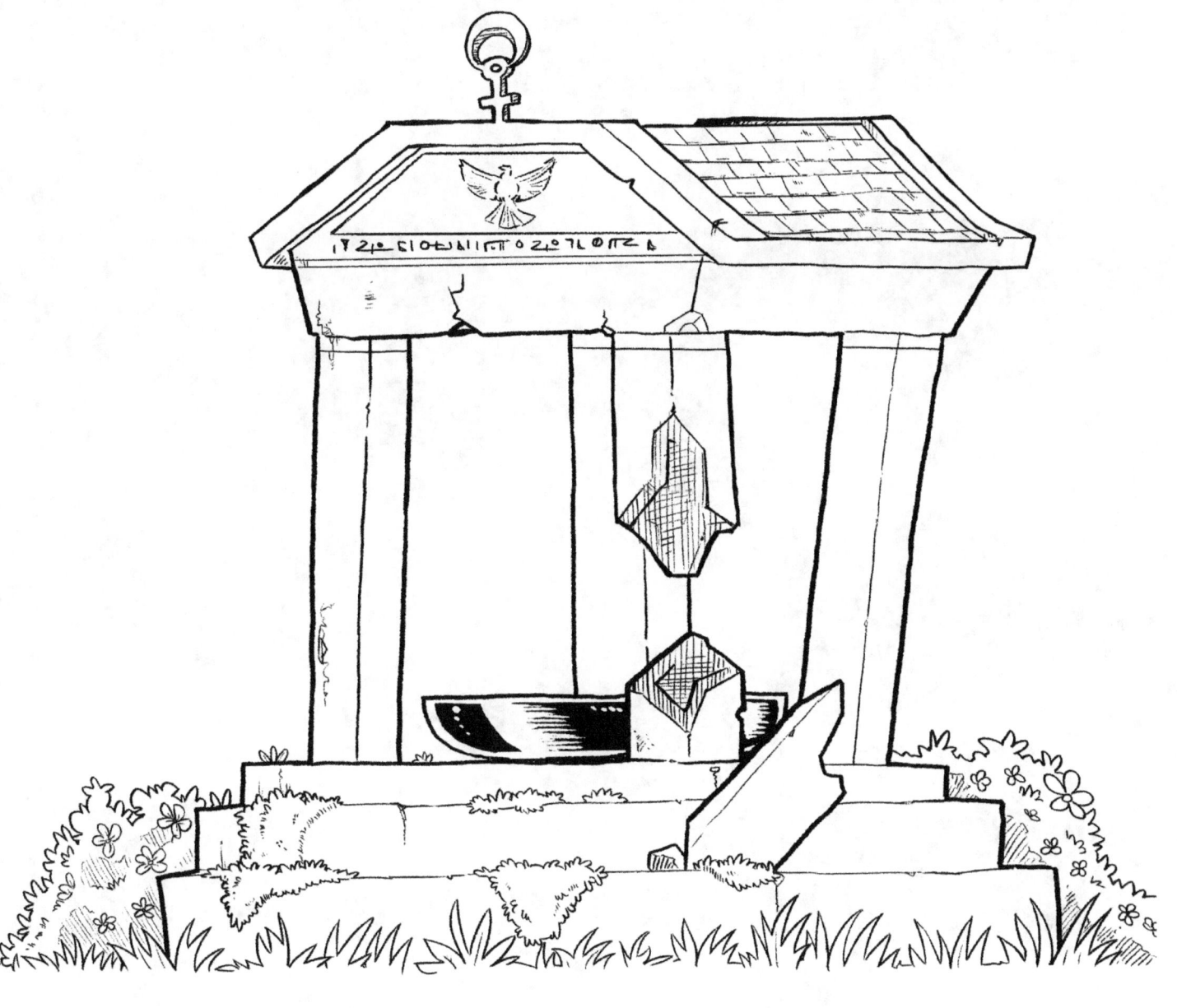

Here lie the remains of a Temple.

The inscription reads:

    Daughter of the Light

      Peace and Love for the Dove

        Drink freely and enjoy this place for you.

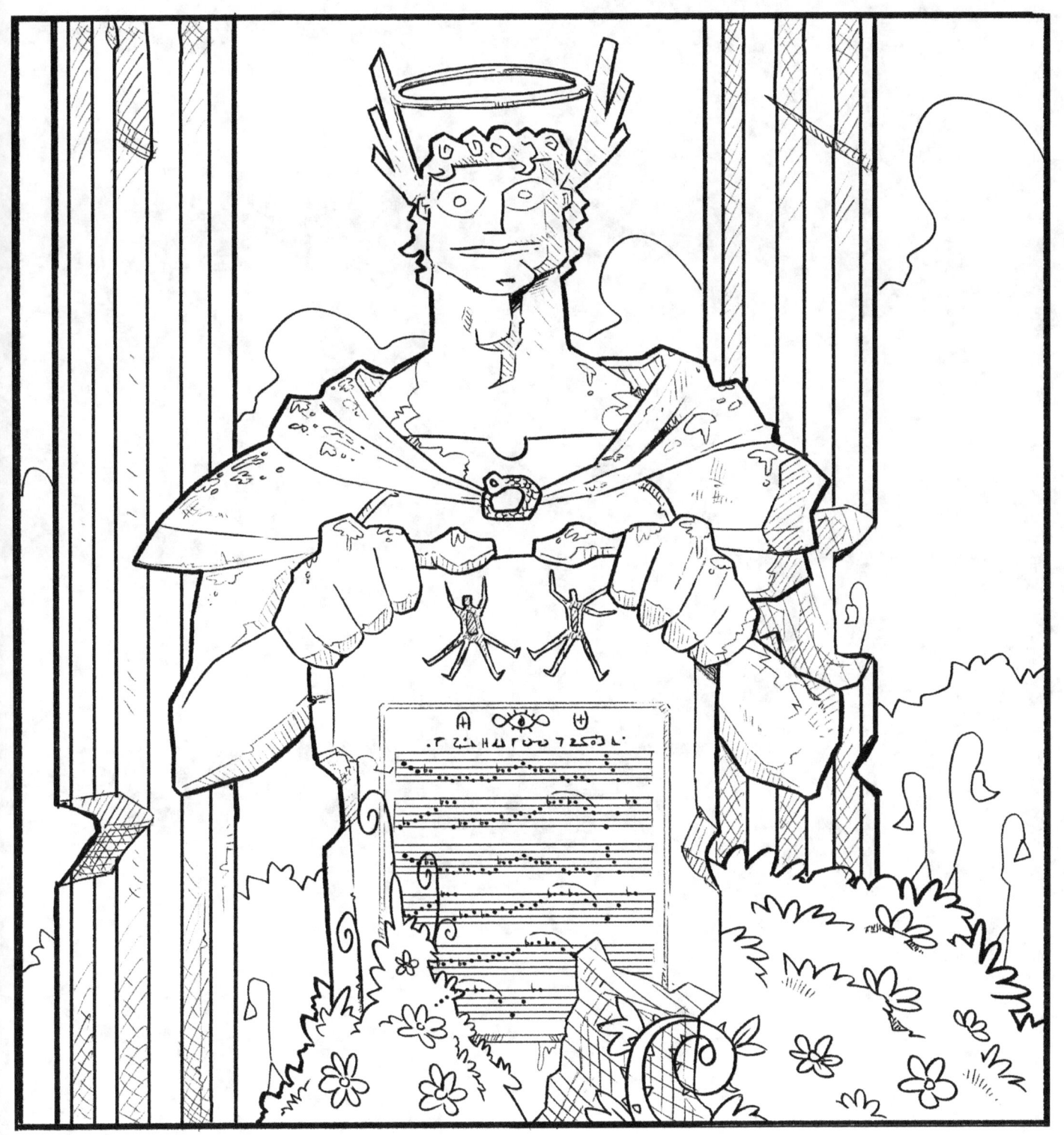

THE INSCRIPTION READS:

A SONG ABOUT BROTHERS.

DEDICATED TO THE MOON, SUN AND THE STARS.

MAY THE ASPECTS BLESS ALL WHO SING.

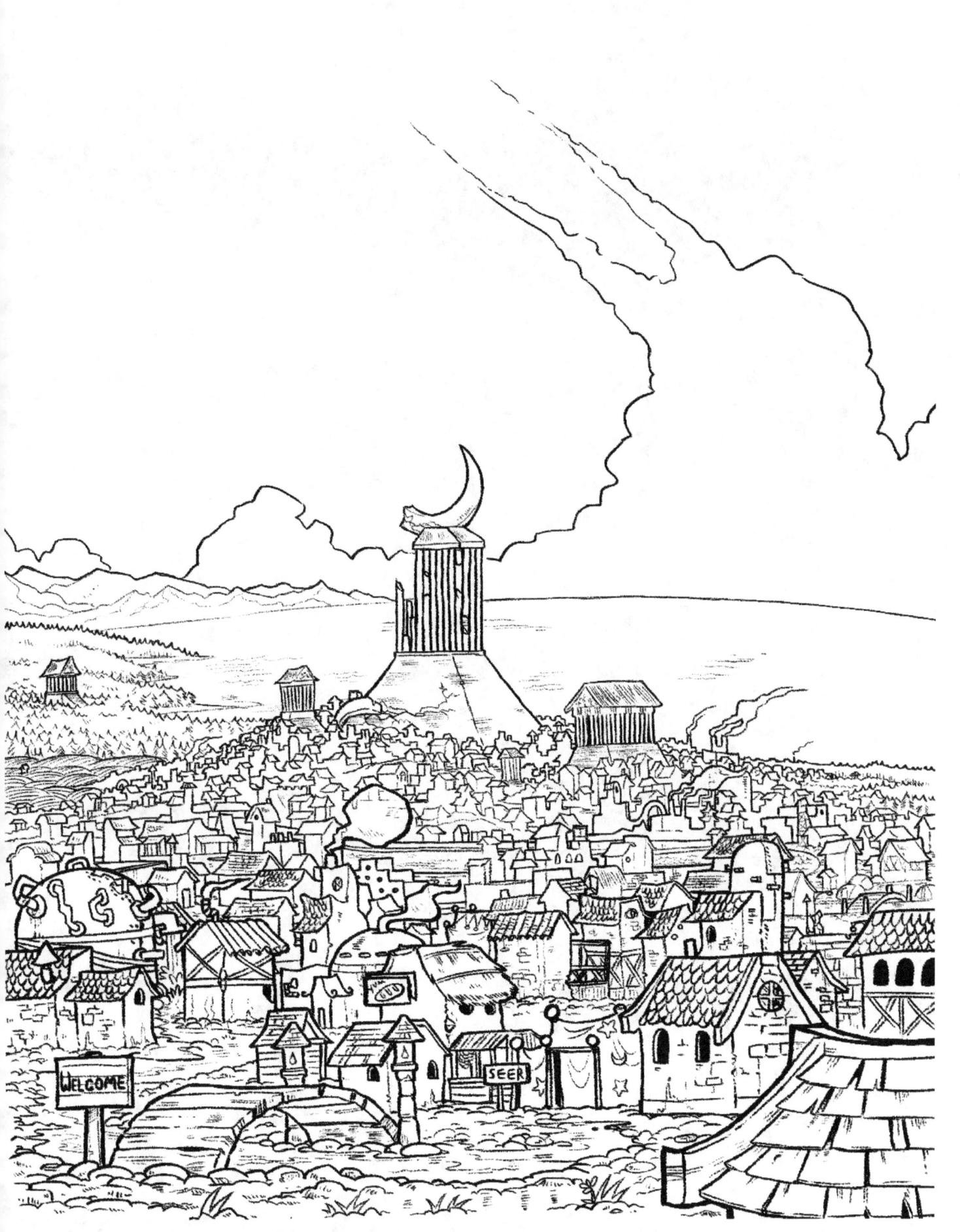

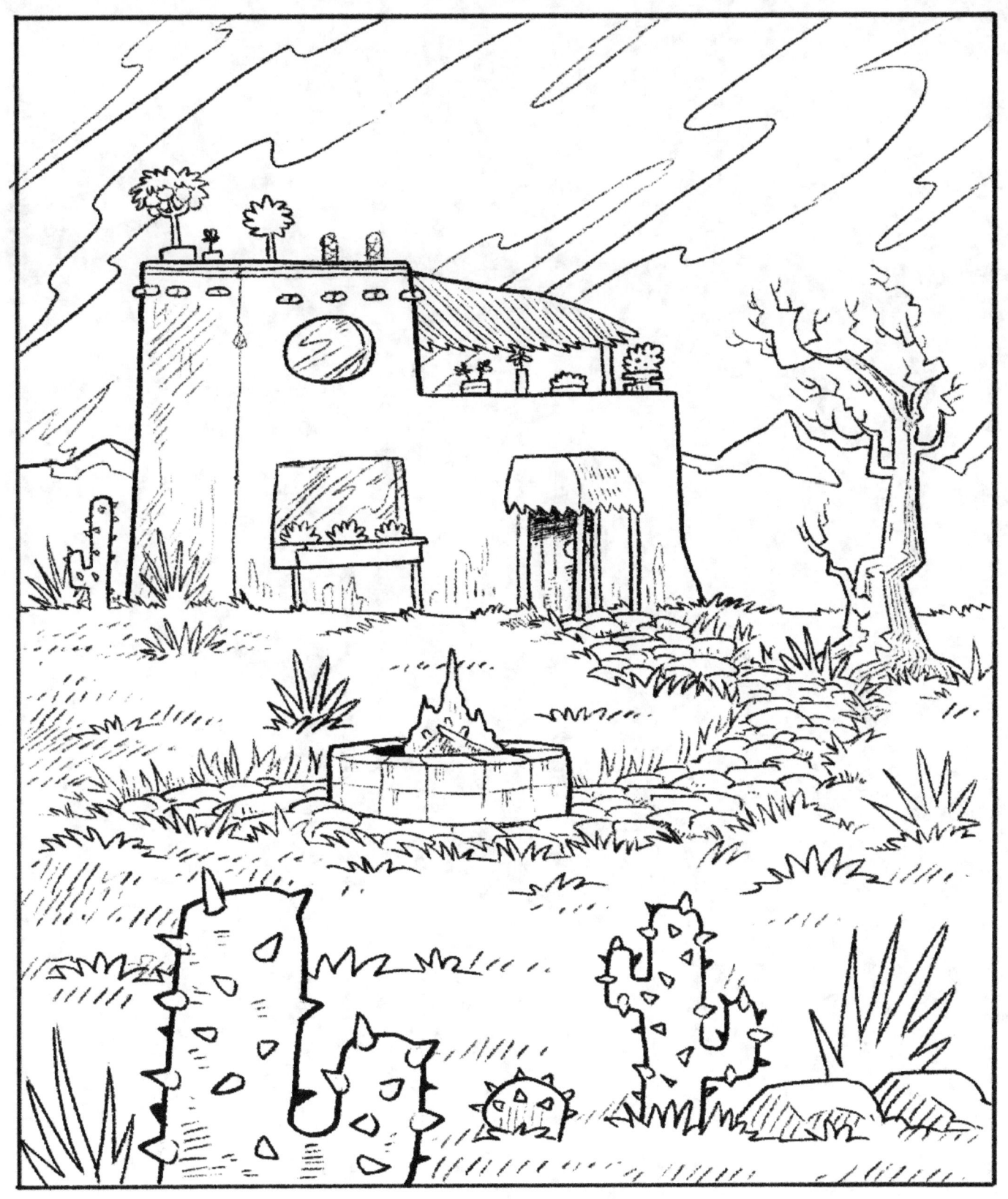

THE PRICKLY PEAR INN

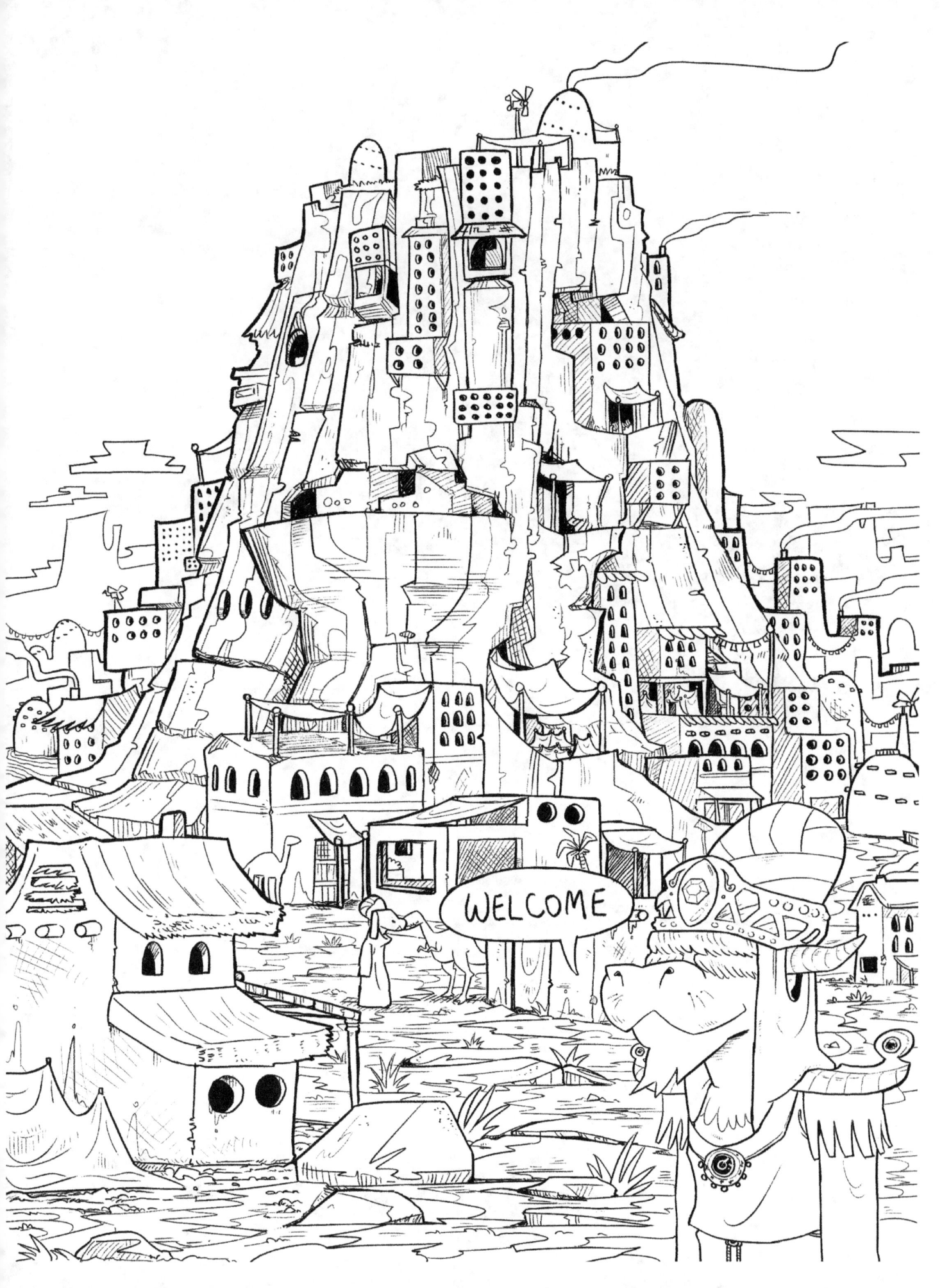

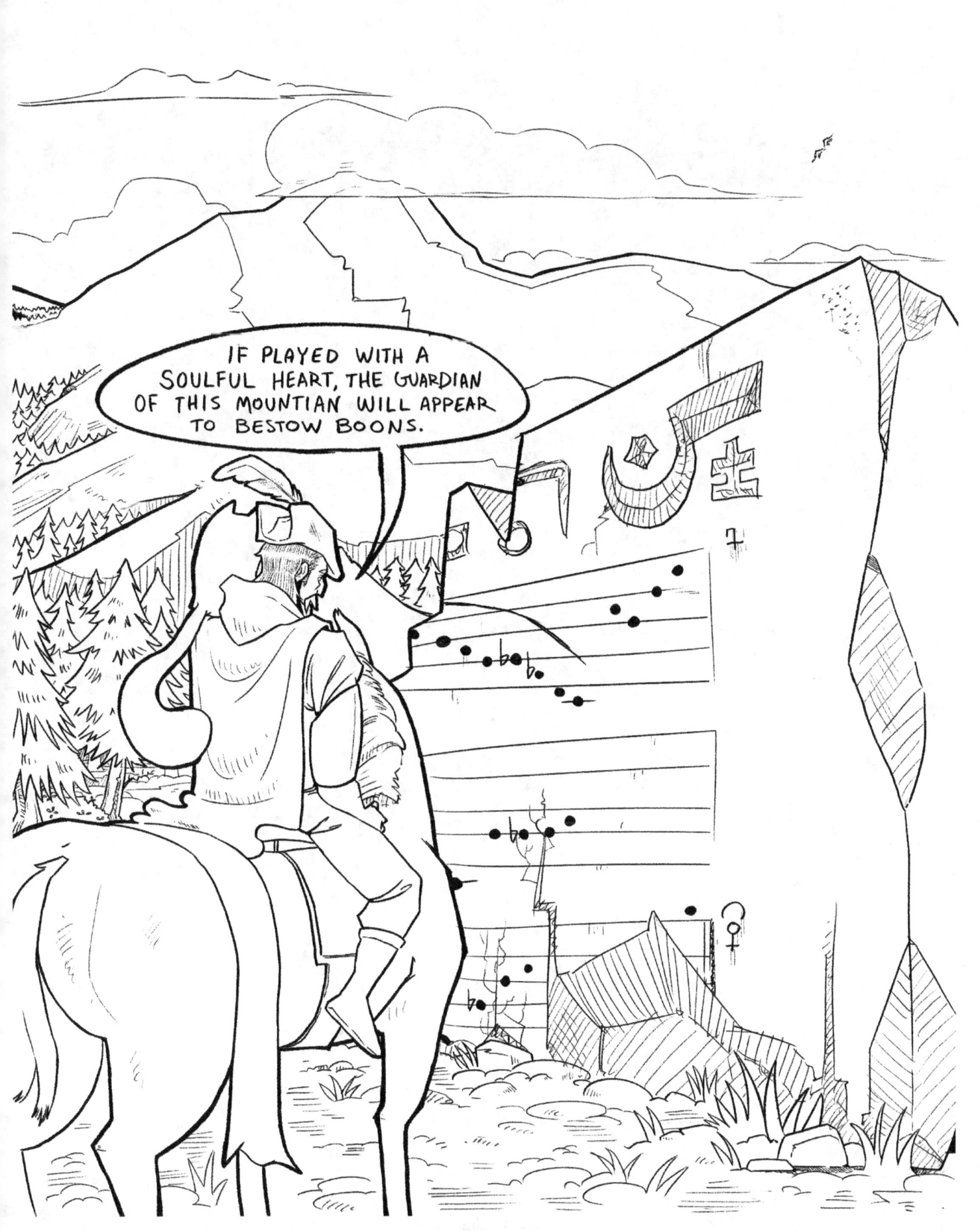

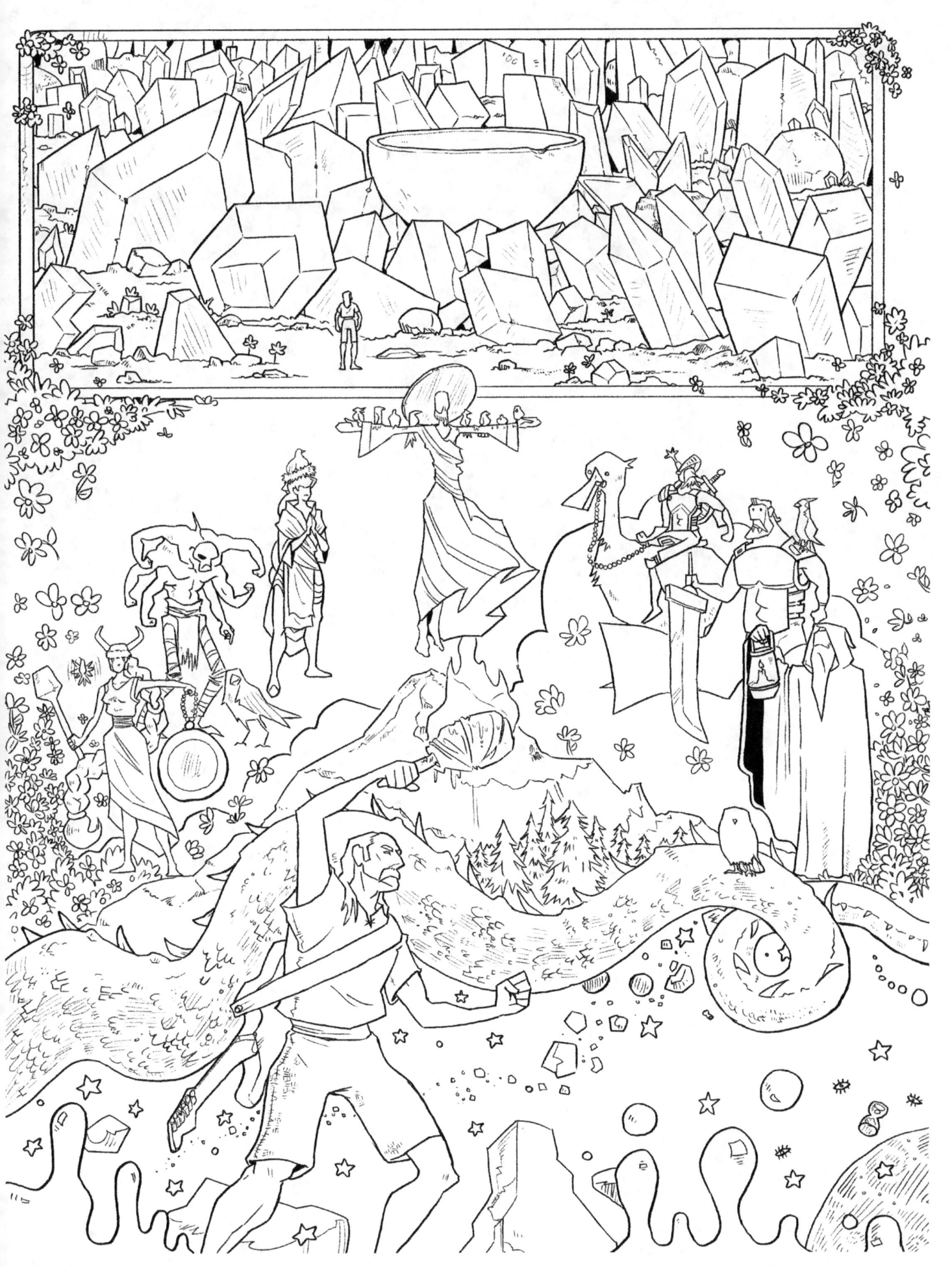

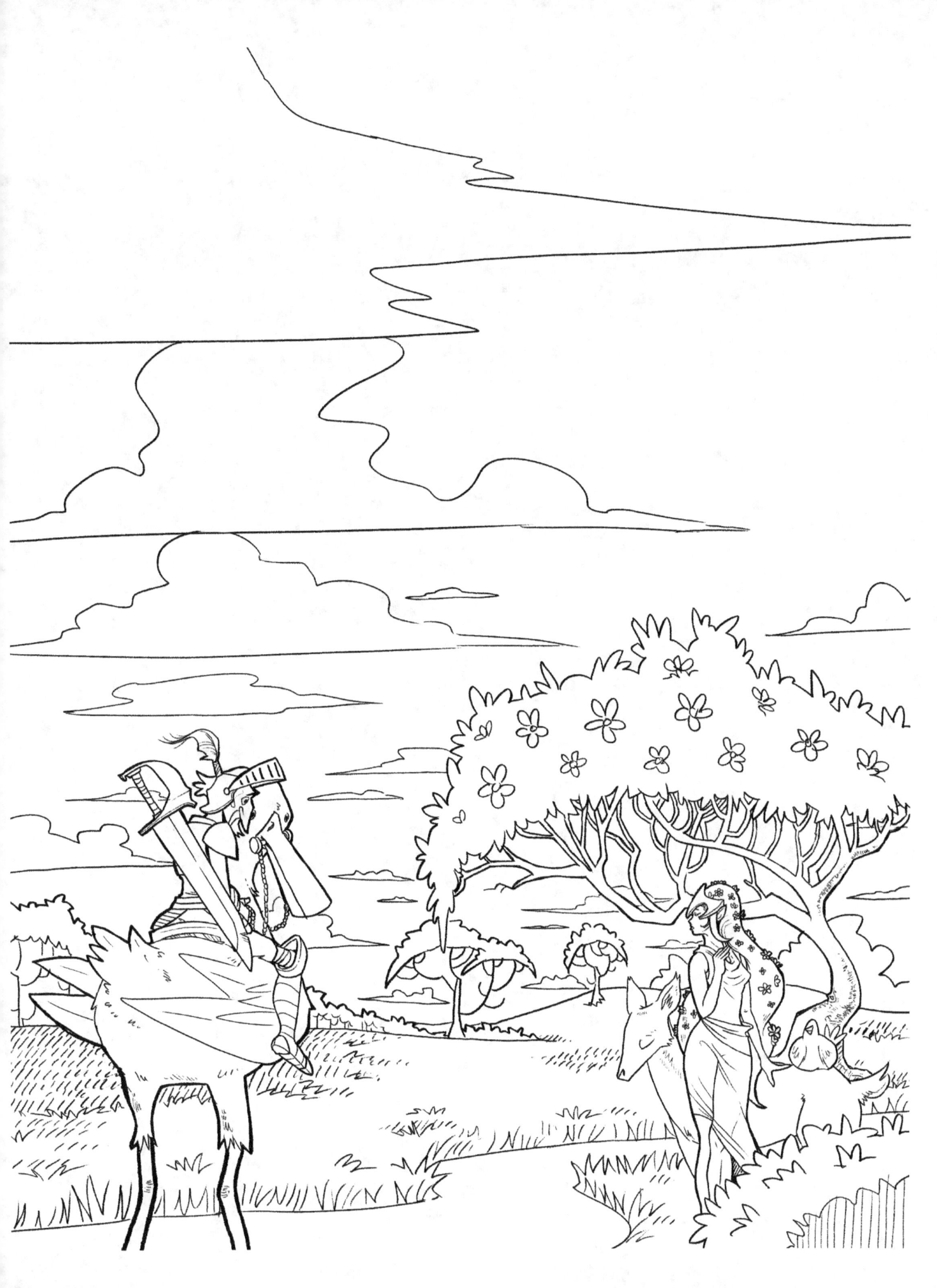

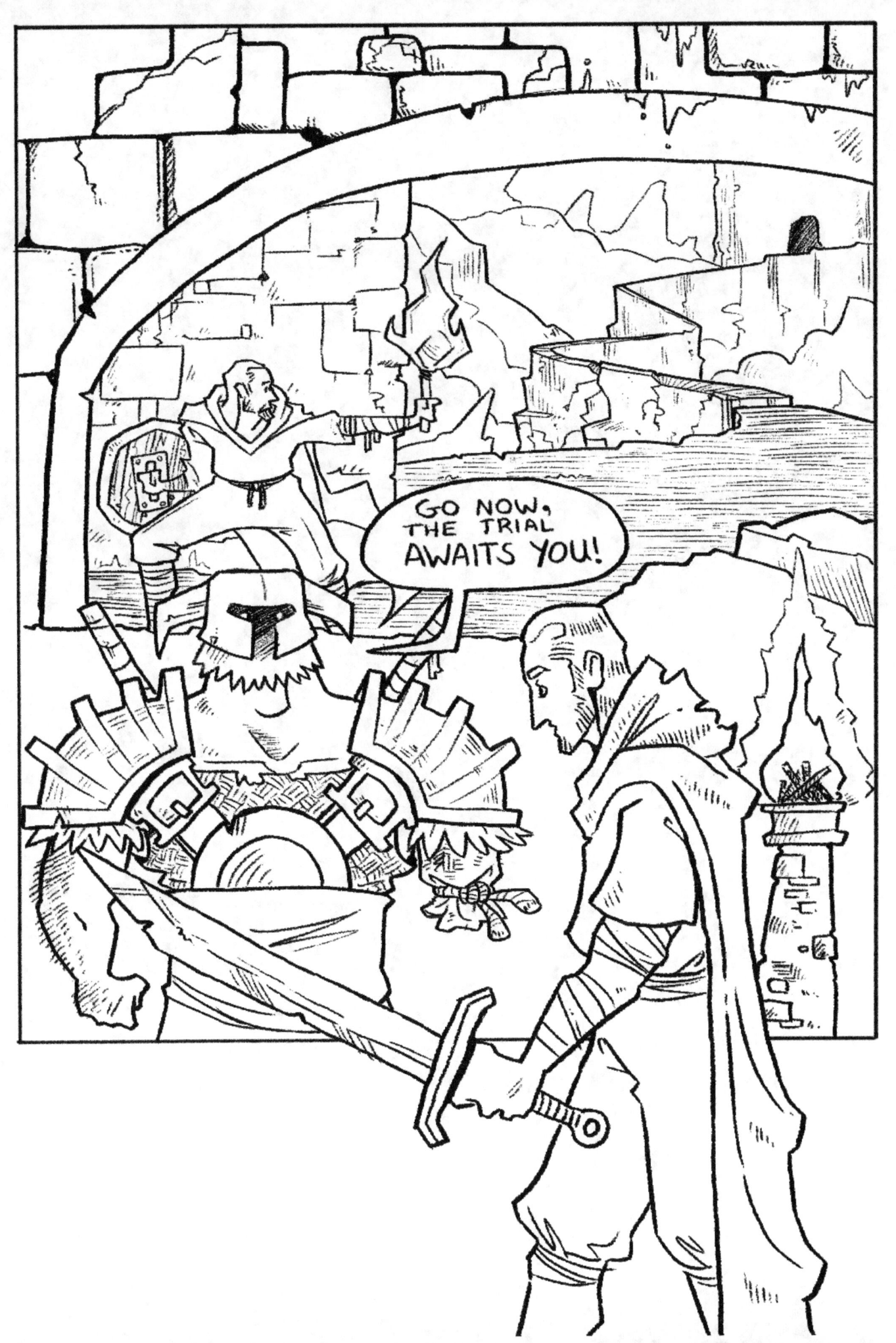

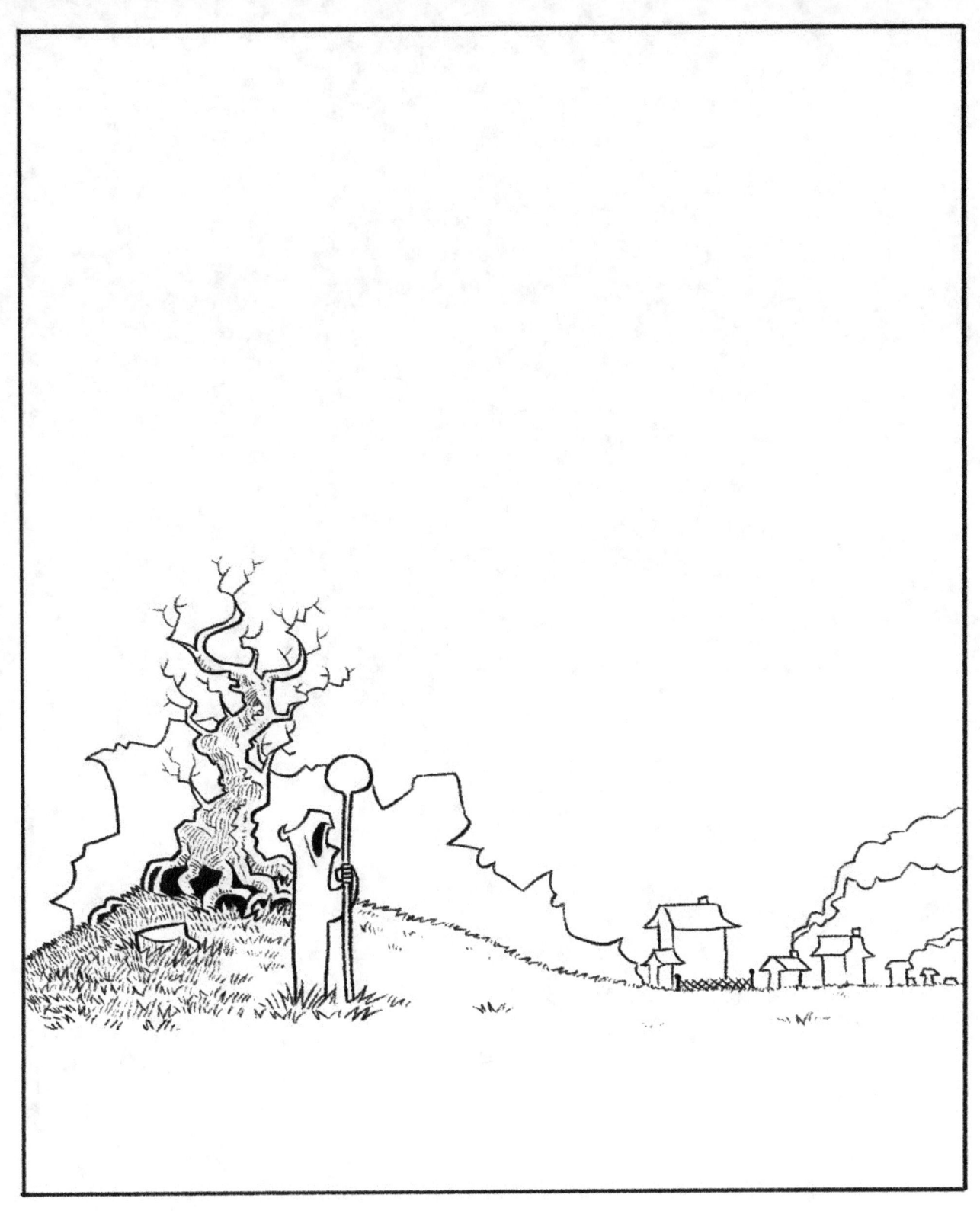

At twiglight on the equinox, If the stars are aligned.
A window opens to another place, mysterious to the Aspects themselves.

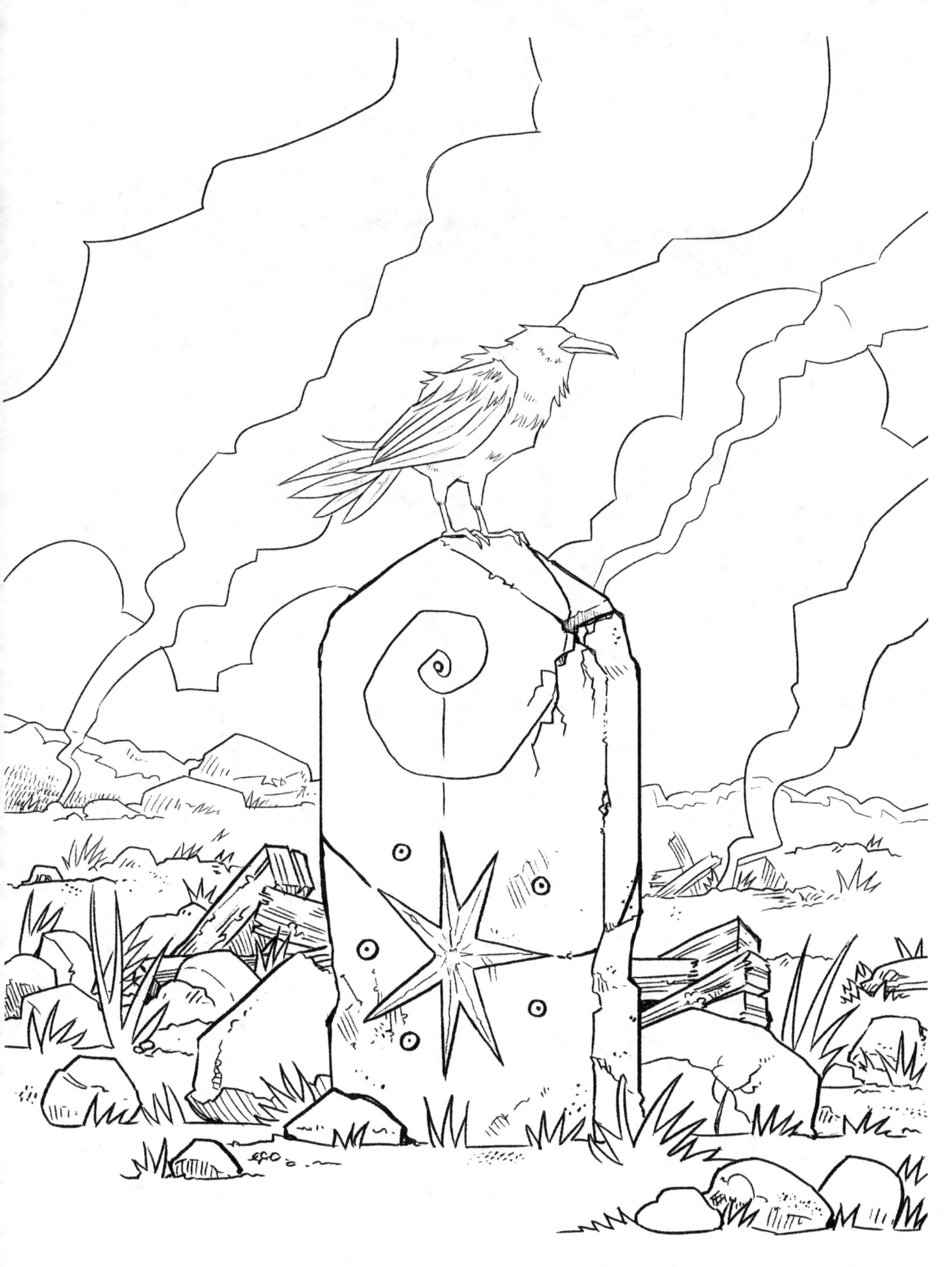

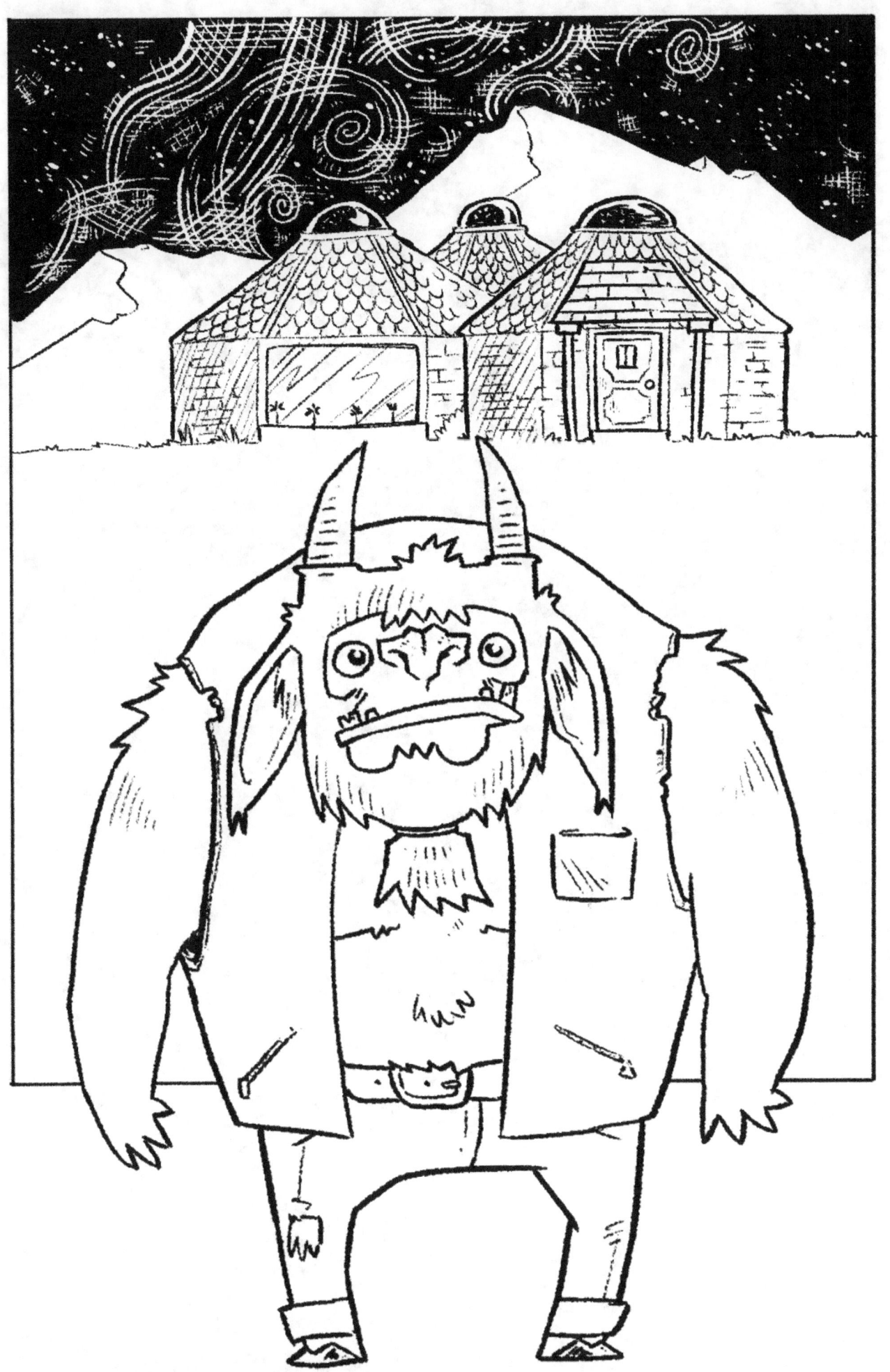

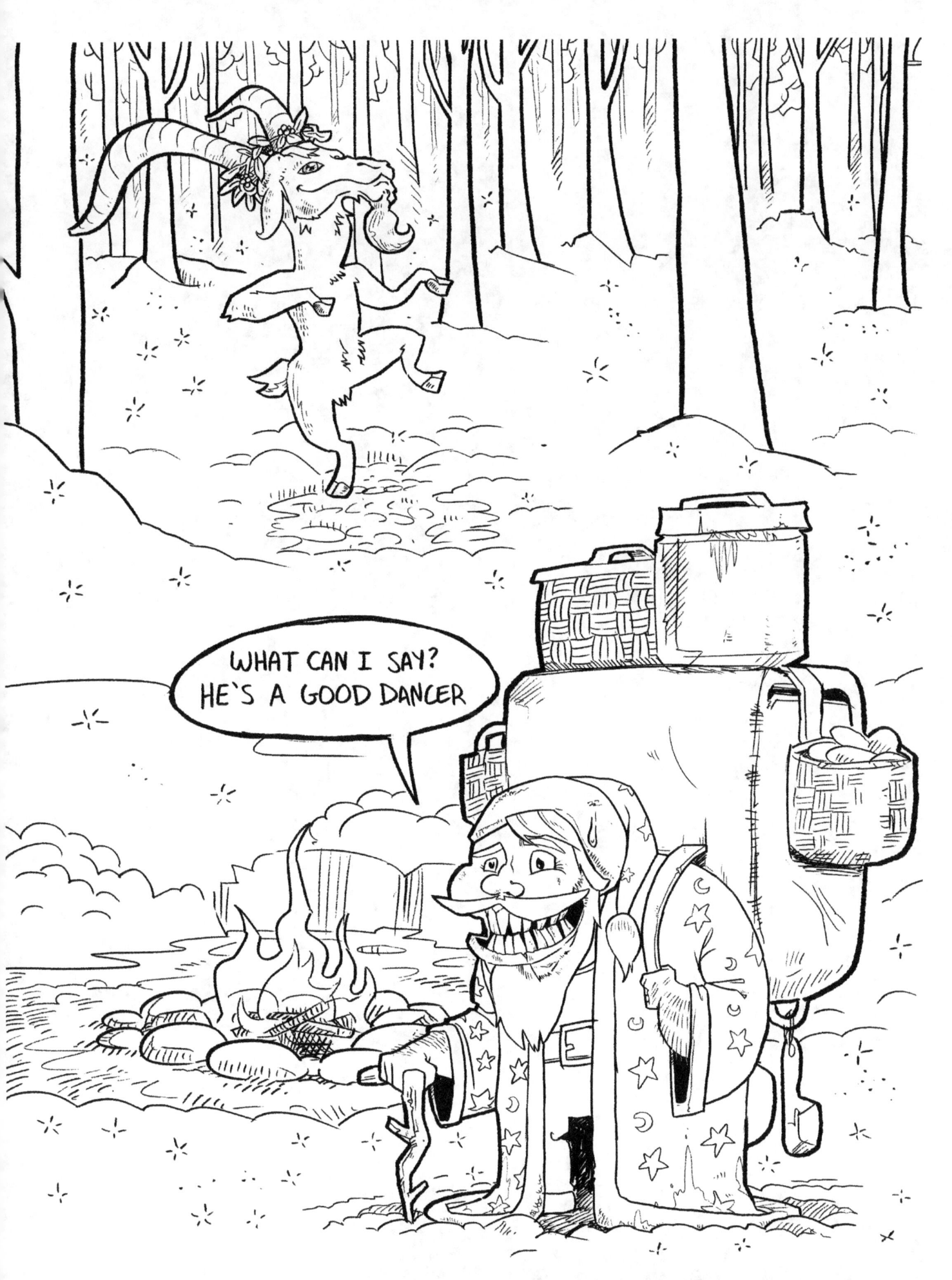

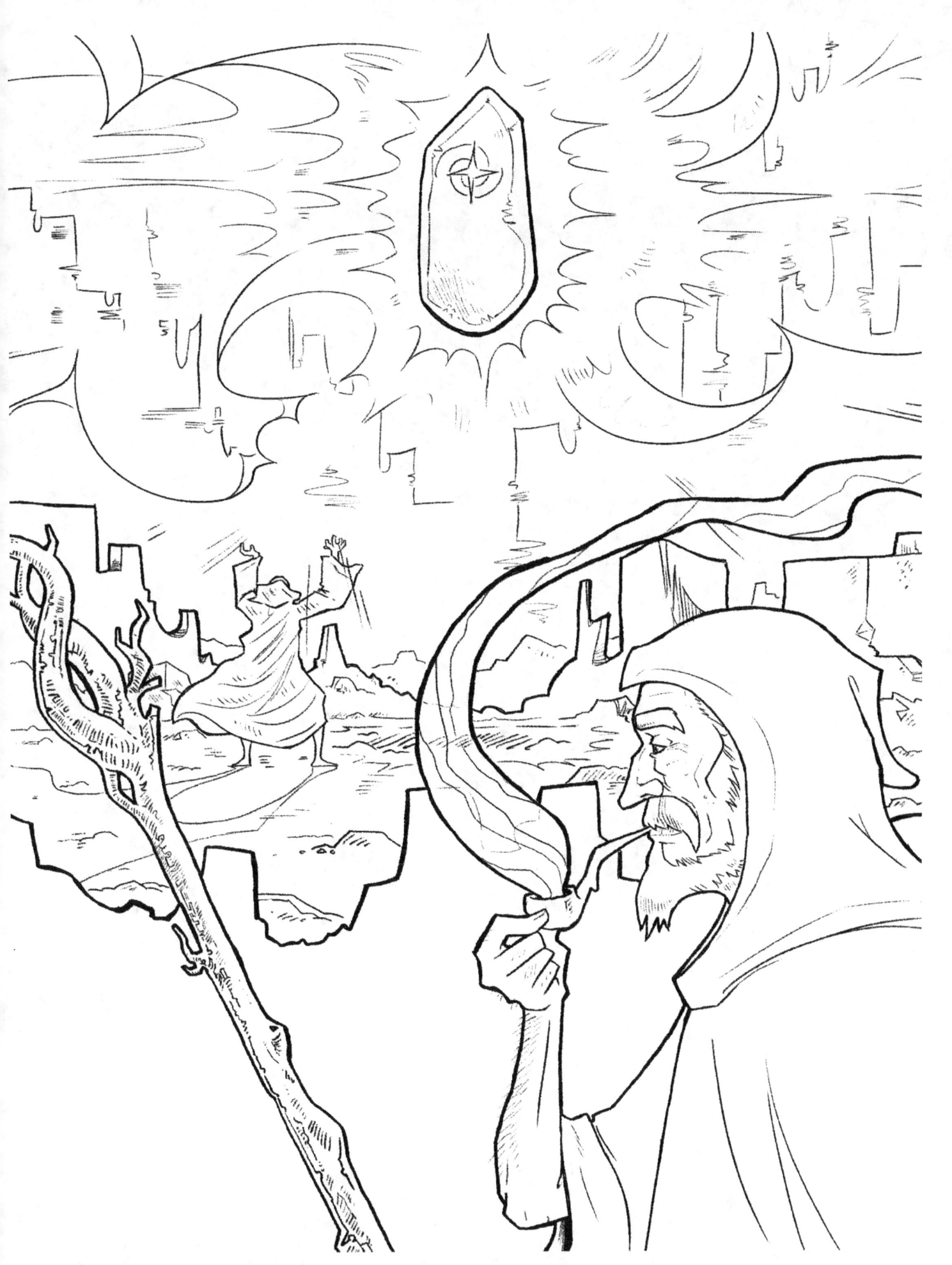

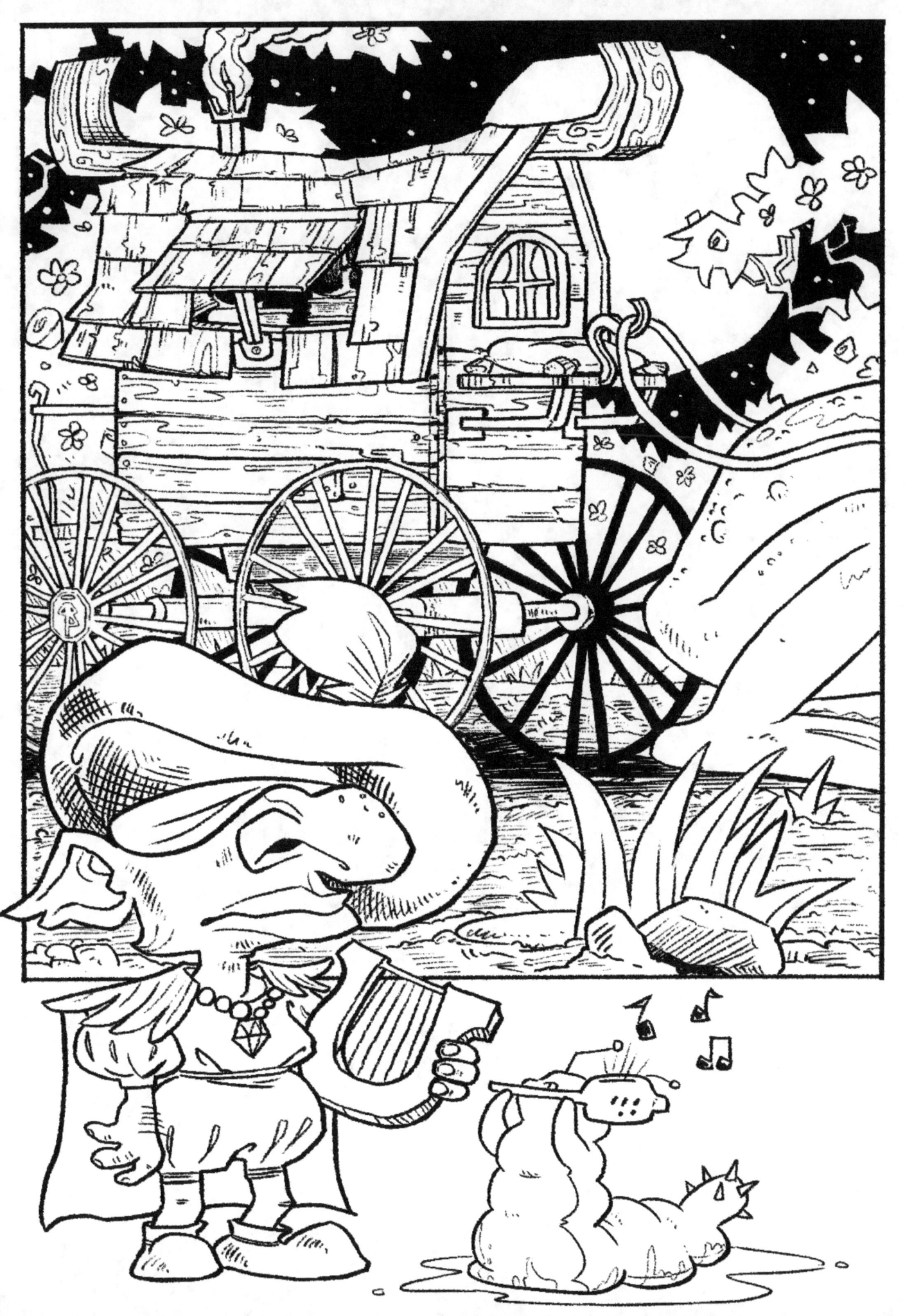

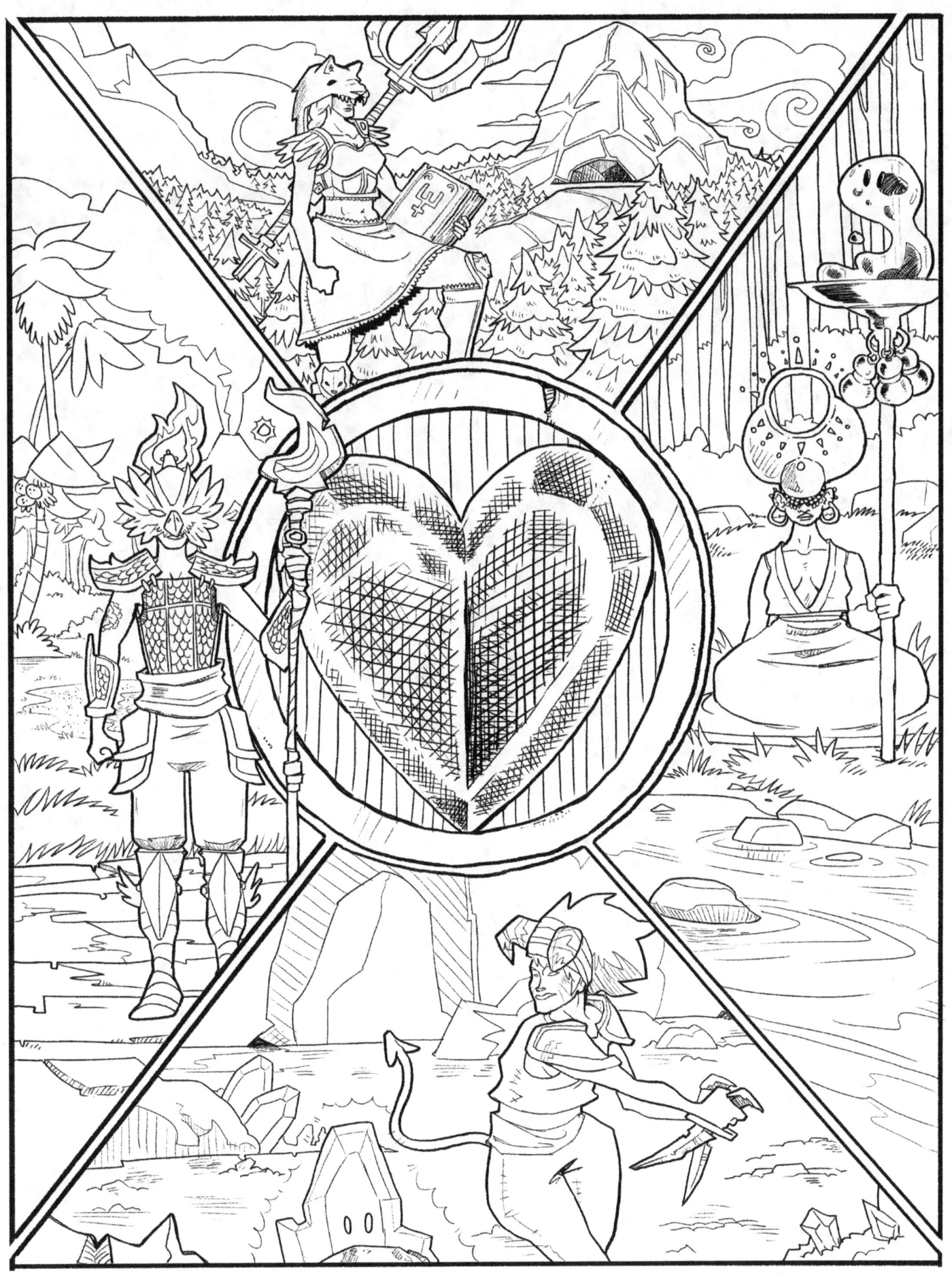

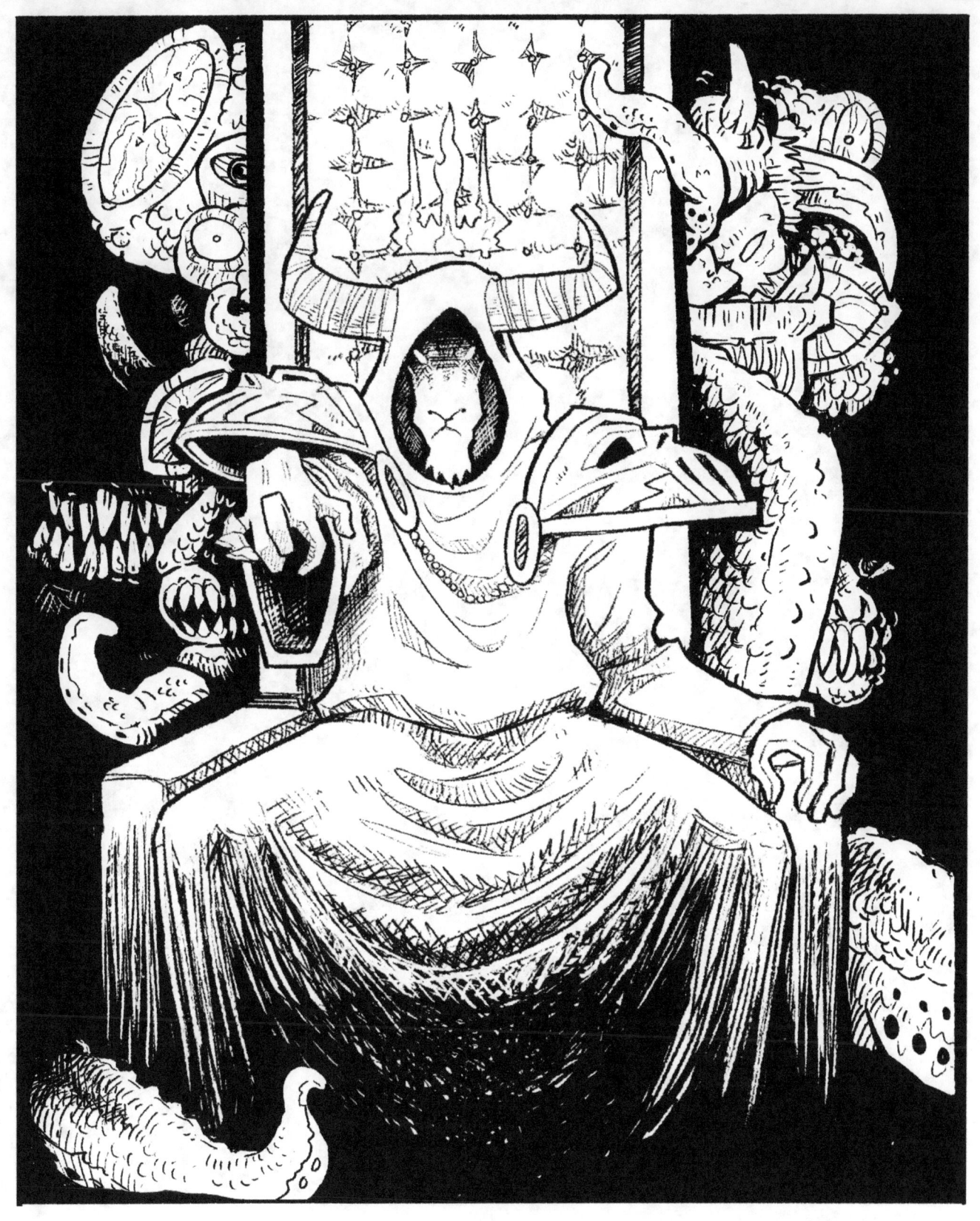

TEMPT THE UNSEEN. GAIN THE WORLD. BUT REMEMBER,

WHEN THE GAME IS DONE, THE PIECES GO BACK IN THE BOX.

Magic,Myth & Monsters Issue #2

Visit fenczikdesign.com and magicmythandmonsters.tumblr.com
for stories, art, music and everything Magic, Myth & Monsters.

Feel free to contact me at stevenfenczik@gmail.com

www.ingramcontent.com/pod-product-compliance
Lightning Source LLC
Chambersburg PA
CBHW081300180526
45170CB00007B/2512